Fashion DRAWING STUDIO

A Guide to Sketching Stylish Fashions

CAPSTONE PRESS
a capstone imprint

TABLE OF CONTENTS

Harajuku

Hollywood

ROCK STAR

SKATER CHIC

Drawing to Design

STEP 1: Start with a simple line drawing. Pick your favorite pose, and use light guidelines to build your model.

STEP 2: Darken the outlines, and start adding in details like hemlines and hand placements.

STEP 3: Erase guidelines, and draw in things such as fabric prints, hair, facial features, and accessories.

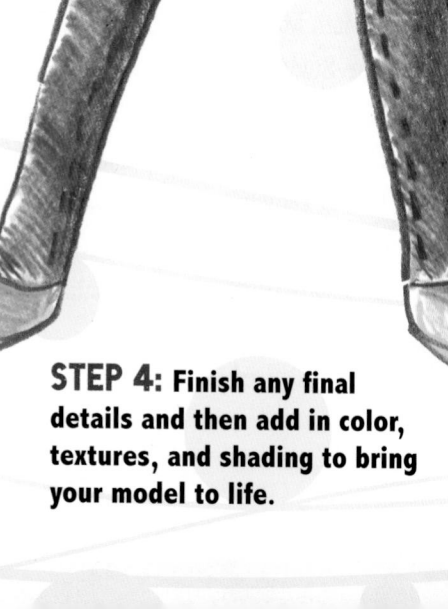

STEP 4: Finish any final details and then add in color, textures, and shading to bring your model to life.

Clothes are more than pieces of fabric used for warmth. Societies around the world and throughout history have used clothing as a statement. Clothing can be used in many ways and for many purposes—as a political statement, for example. Clothing is also used to express the customs and culture of local people. It represents changing times or events from the past. And it can be beautiful.

Fashion can be as simple as a popular look, like Girly Girl. It can represent the style of a country or region, like All-American Girl or Harajuku. It can show off a person's interests, like Skater Chic. It can give us a glimpse into the lives of the rich and famous, like Rock Star and Hollywood.

Fashion illustrators use their talents to show off the latest clothing styles and designs. But fashion illustration is also a form of artistic expression. The colors, lines, shapes, and techniques used are unique to each illustrator. Whether a quick runway sketch or a full-color drawing used for an advertisement, a talented illustrator can bring a model to life.

As you flip through the pages of this book, think of how you can add your own personal style. Draw the models your way. Use what art style works best for you. Invent your own fabrics, textures, and prints. Don't forget—these are fun fashions YOU can sketch!

Follow these tips for a fun fashion experience:

- Sketching allows you to make any major changes before adding color or details. Ink pens will give your sketches a more finished look.
- Experiment with different art mediums. Marker and colored pencil are fun, but don't forget about watercolor paints and pencils, pastels, permanent markers, and charcoals.
- Give digital art a try. There are many free or inexpensive apps for smartphones or tablets.
- Adding 3-D effects, such as glue, glitter, rhinestones, and collage, will help your art pop.
- Use what you draw! Hold an art show to show off your pieces. Or, better yet, bring your outfits to life and have a fashion show with your friends.

Sweet Simplicity

A sweet sweater and cute capris are a great look for any all-American girl. The trick is turning an everyday outfit into something flirty and feminine.

TIP: Don't go overboard with this one. Pair your favorite girly print with simple, solid colors.

Coordinated Couture

Suit up for style with an all-American girl twist. Pencil skirts are timeless—make yours modern with bright colors and patterns. A jacket with a wide collar draws the eye to a confident girl who's going places.

TIP: While matching is great, you don't want to overdo it. Pair a coordinated outfit with a flashy purse that complements your chosen colors.

—Dip-Dyed Diva—

Can't make it to the tropics? Bring the summer sun to you! Warm tones give a tiered dress an exotic look and a bright splash of color. Cool things off with a crocheted jacket and some sharp boots.

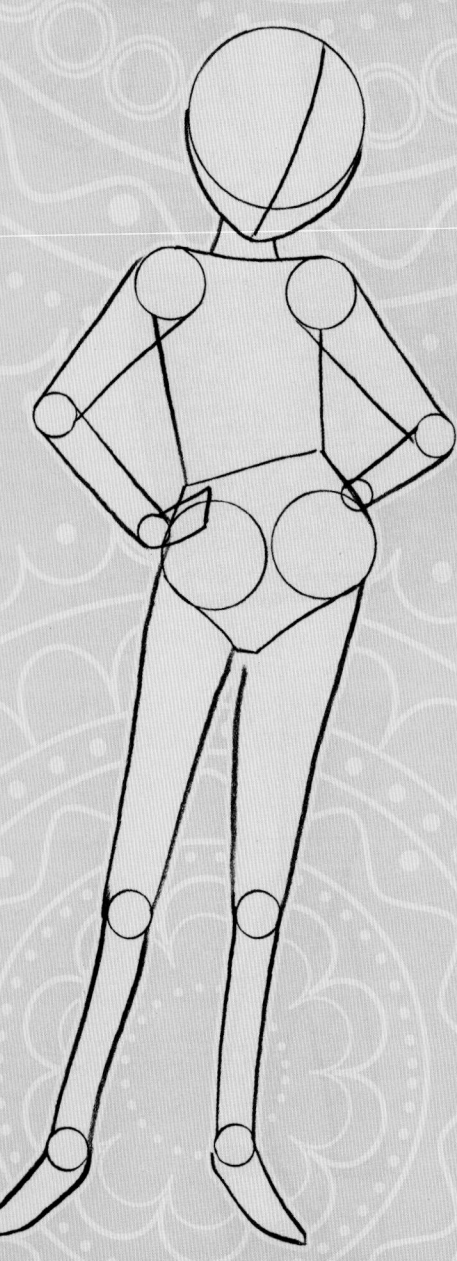

TIP: Try using a single color to create different layers and shades to the dress.

The Great American Outdoors

Explore the great American outdoors and look good doing it! Choose soft plaids and familiar shorts for comfort and style. Stash accessories in a stylish yet rugged rucksack.

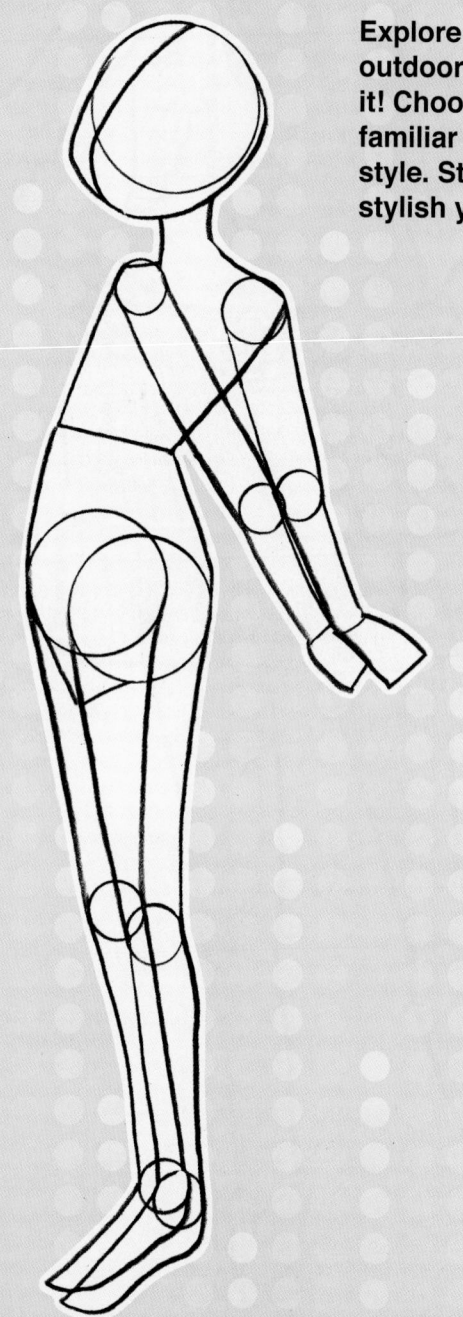

TIP: Plaids come in all colors and patterns. Experiment with a variety of prints and styles to find your favorite.

NEW WEST

Turn the Old West into something new. A trendy tank cinched with a glittering rhinestone belt is a start. But adding a cowboy hat, a hot handbag, and some blingy conchos will show how the West was won.

TIP: Don't be afraid of the Wild West. Fringe, ruffles, distressed denim, leather, vests, and boots are only a few style additions to bring to this outfit.

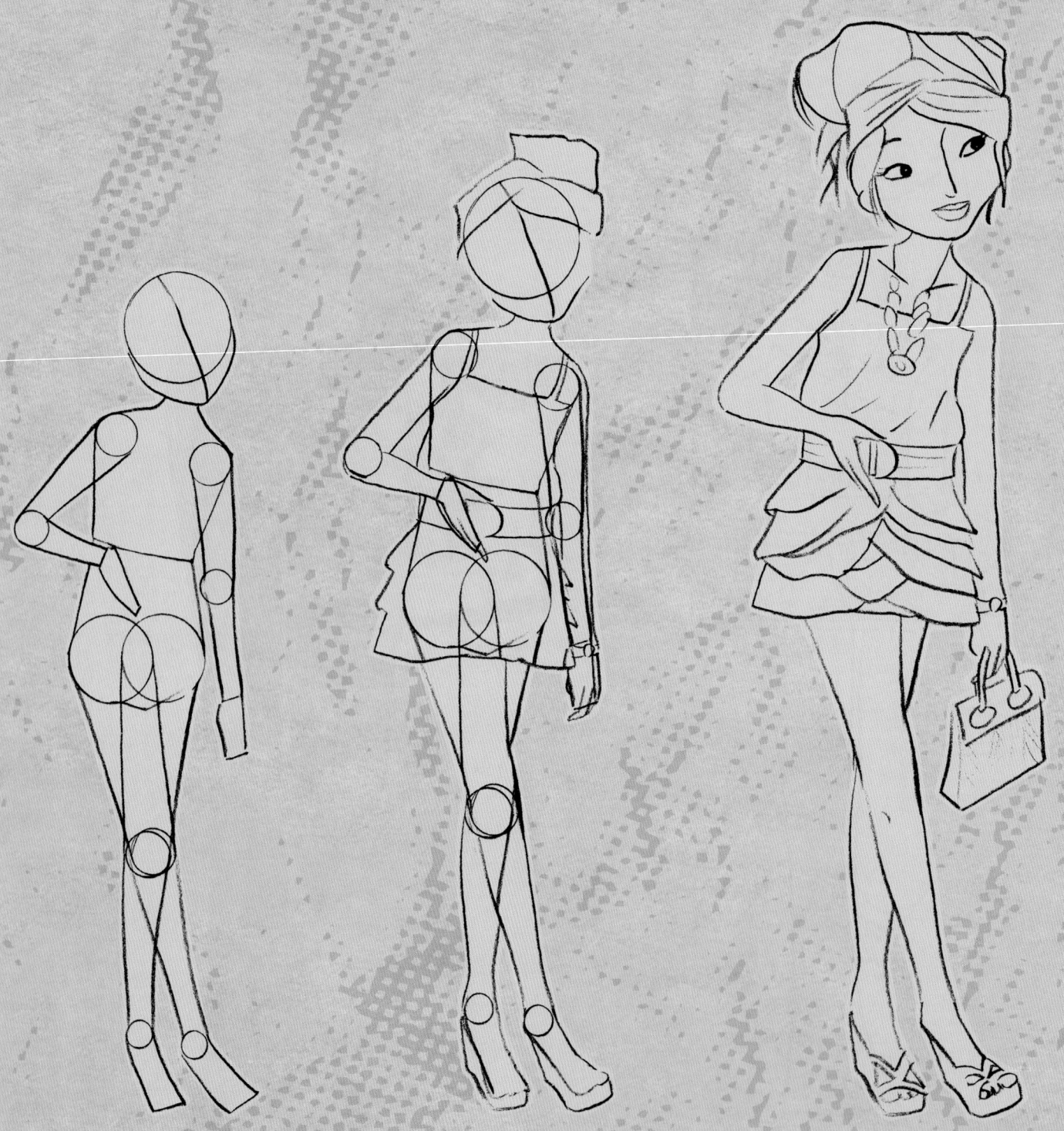

Natural Earth Tones

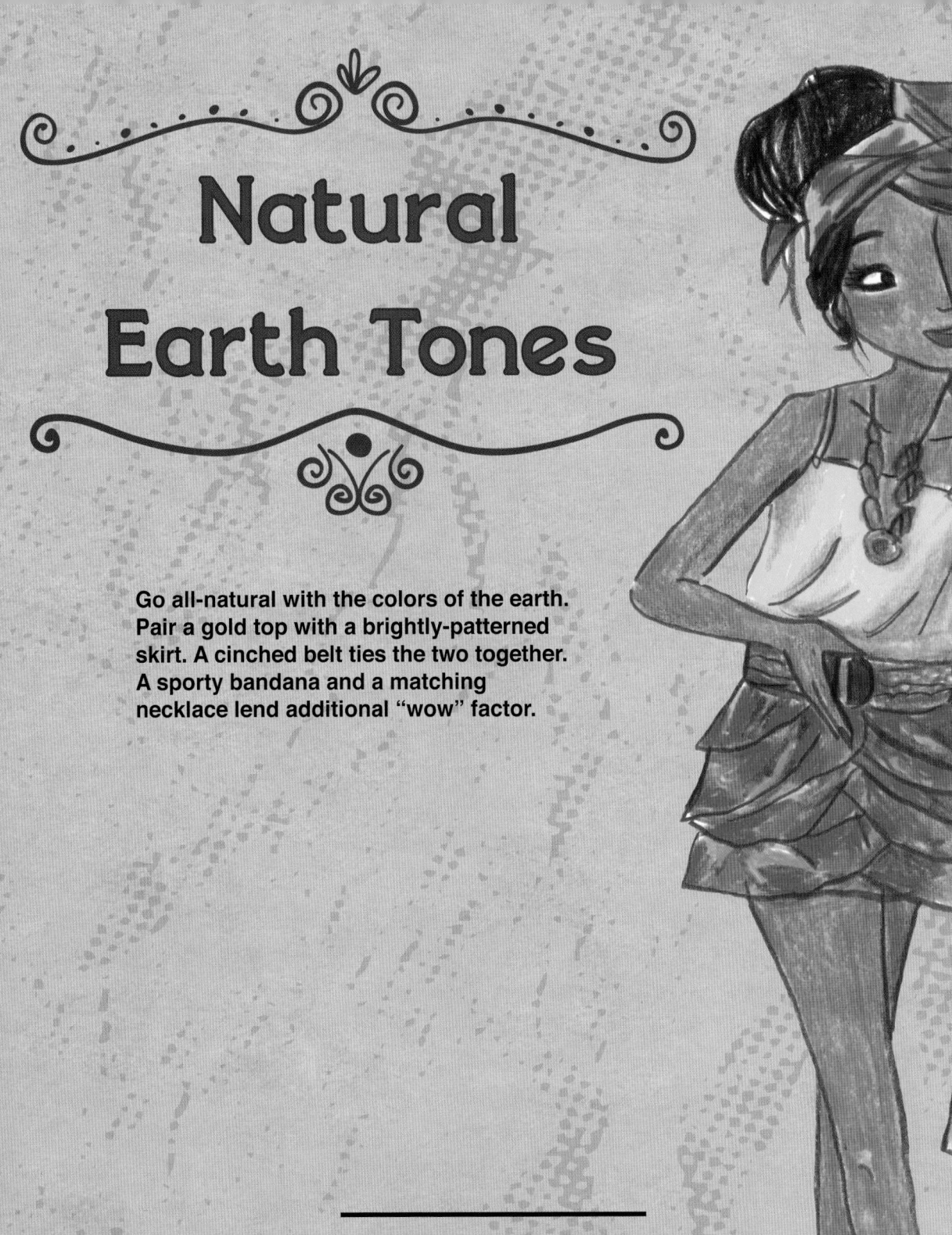

Go all-natural with the colors of the earth. Pair a gold top with a brightly-patterned skirt. A cinched belt ties the two together. A sporty bandana and a matching necklace lend additional "wow" factor.

TIP: Experiment with color! Figure out which colors complement each other and which colors clash.

HOME TEAM

Do you run the bases or watch from the sidelines? Use America's pastime as fashion inspiration and you're always a winner. The crowd will be rooting for the home team!

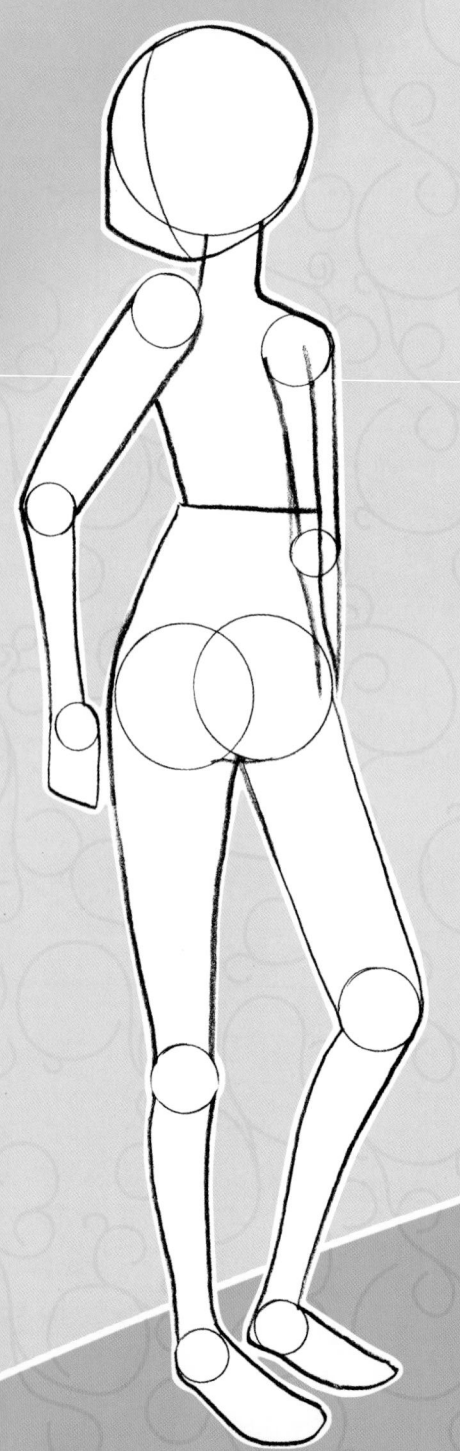

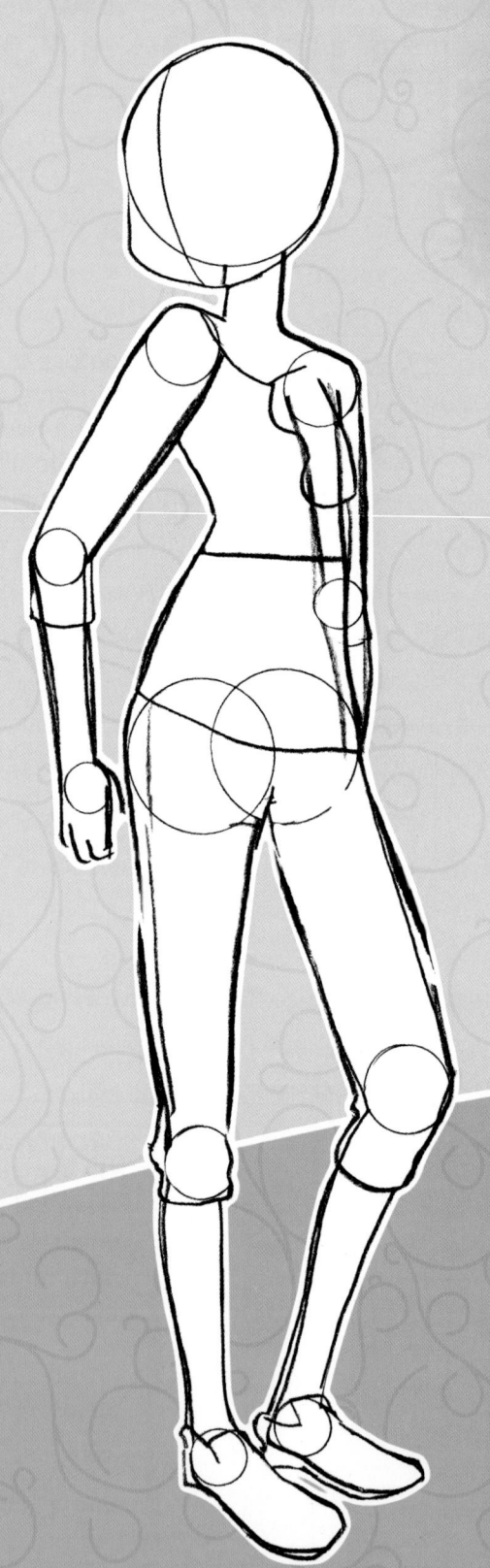

TIP: Nothing says baseball like pinstripes. Use light pencil lines to create this traditional print for an even more authentic baseball feel.

An Ono Outfit

When a Hawaiian says something is "ono," you know it's good! Get inspired by Waikiki beach and dress yourself in an ono outfit.

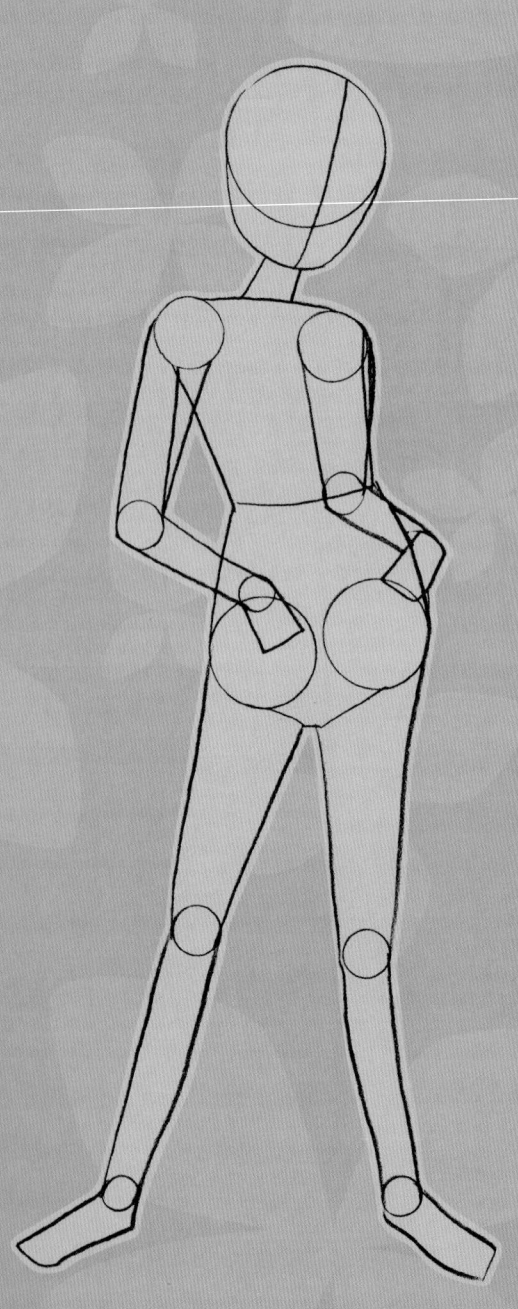

Got It Covered

The all-American girl is always trendy and chic. A flowing top and wide-leg bottoms are both cool and comfortable. Pair them with a shimmering scarf, flashy wedges, and a flowery handbag for an all-day outfit.

TIP: Embroidery is a great way to add color and dimension to clothing. Make short, dark lines with a colored pencil to represent embroidery stitches.

college COOl

Show the world who you cheer for with your own twist on college style. Stripes, pleats, and argyle are classic combinations for the college-minded fashionista.

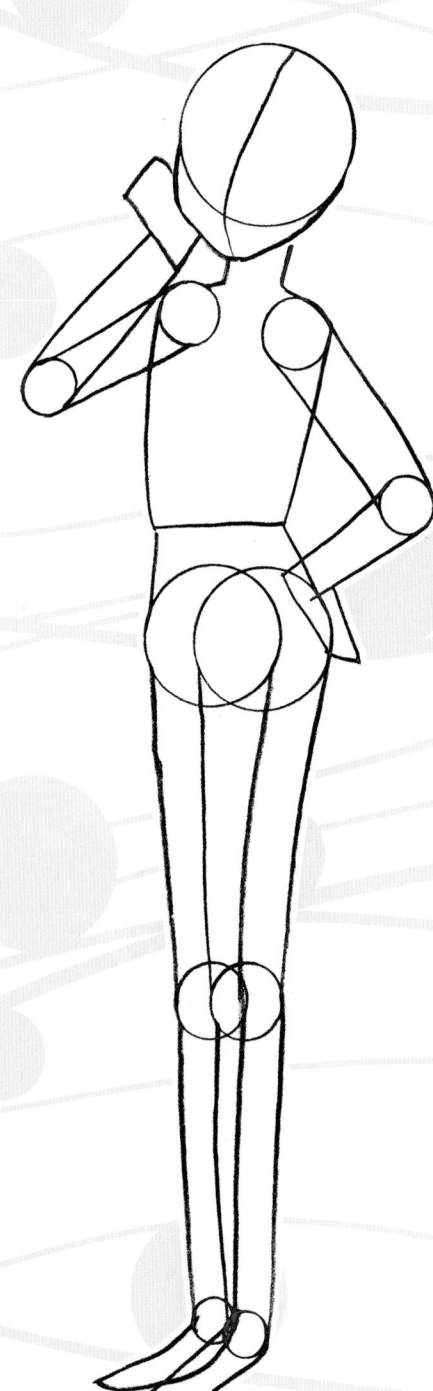

TIP: Scarves, foam fingers, pom-poms, and banners are great accessory additions.

Southwest Seasoning

Take in some of the American southwest with rich, natural colors. Native prints, denim accessories, and a touch of amber will spice up any outfit.

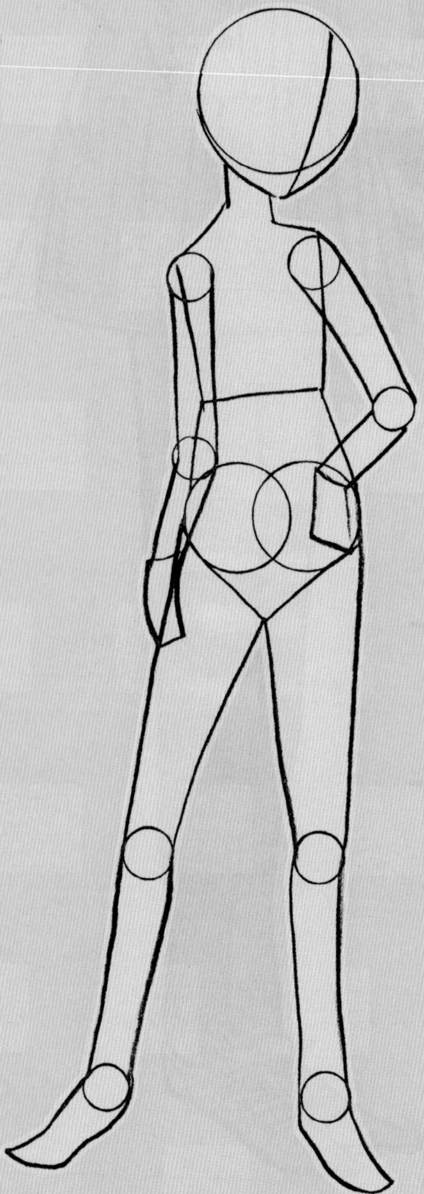

TIP: Get inspired! Explore traditional Mexican and American Indian prints for fresh pattern ideas.

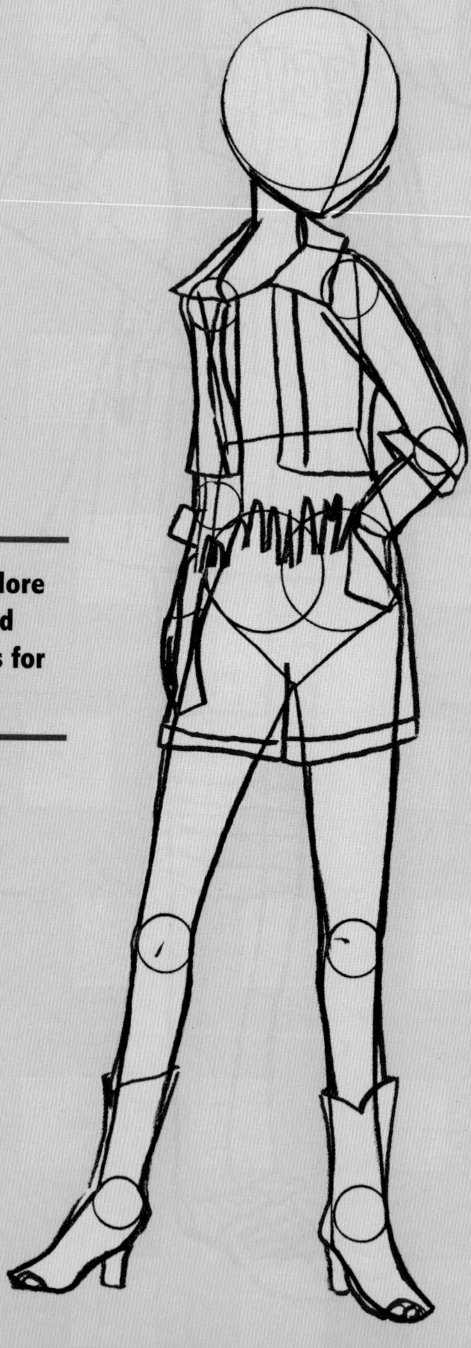

INFLUENTIAL PRINTS

Nothing's hotter than African-inspired clothing added to the all-American girl's closet. Sophisticated yet subtle, traditional prints are brought into the next generation of fashion.

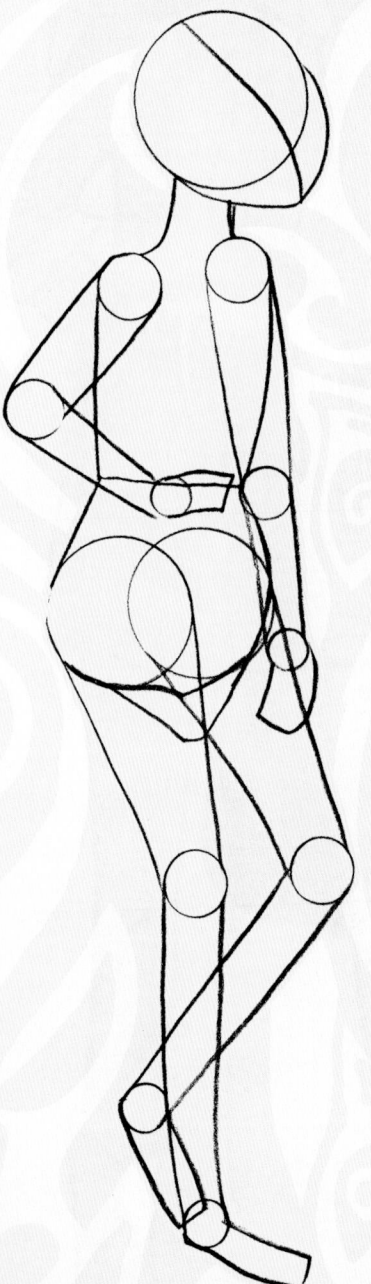

TIP: Use a mixture of hot and cool colors and geometric shapes to create a one-of-a-kind print that shows off your style.

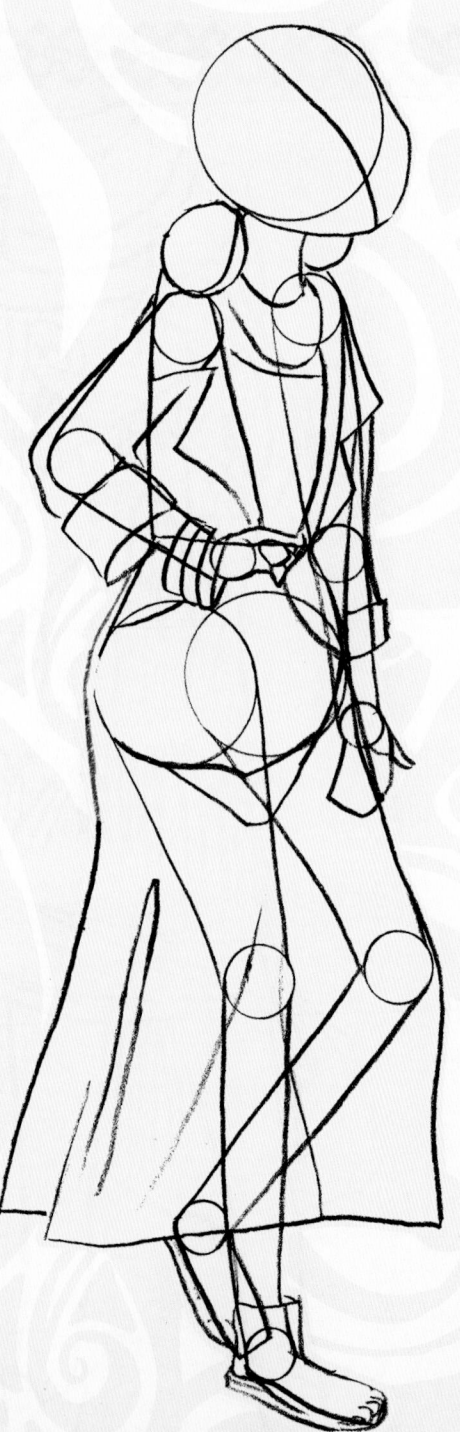

Embroidered Edges

A simple tiered dress is accented with a splash of color and some oversized accessories. Color is minimized, keeping the focus on the dress.

TIP: Use a toothpick or the end of a paintbrush to paint the dots on the dress.

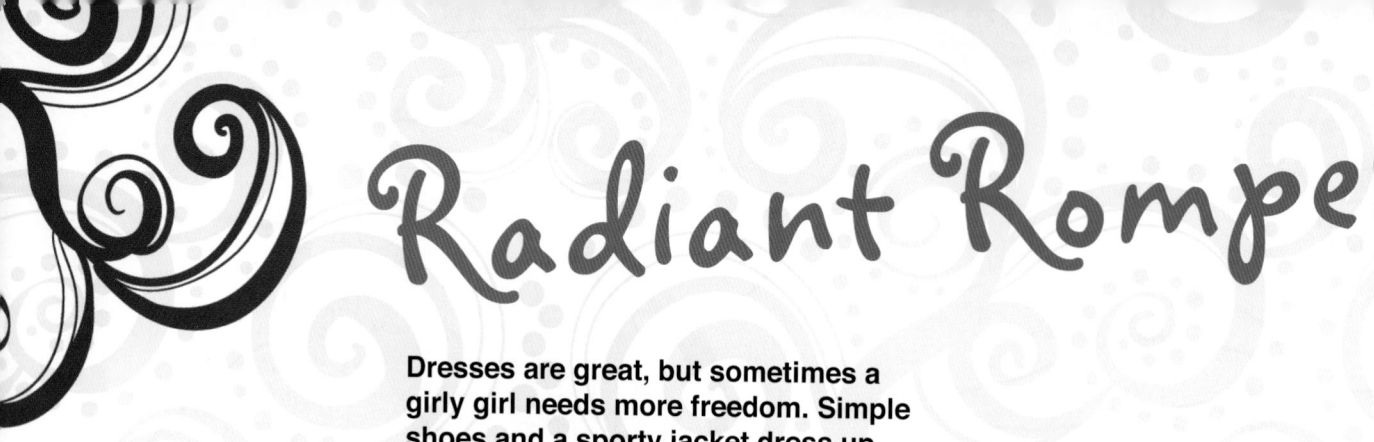

Radiant Romper

Dresses are great, but sometimes a girly girl needs more freedom. Simple shoes and a sporty jacket dress up this radiant romper.

TIP: Use marker over a dry watercolor base to copy the romper's floral pattern.

BEACH BOUTIQUE

Take your wardrobe on vacation by turning it tropical. An off-the-shoulder peasant shirt and belted denim shorts are the perfect pair for poolside lounging.

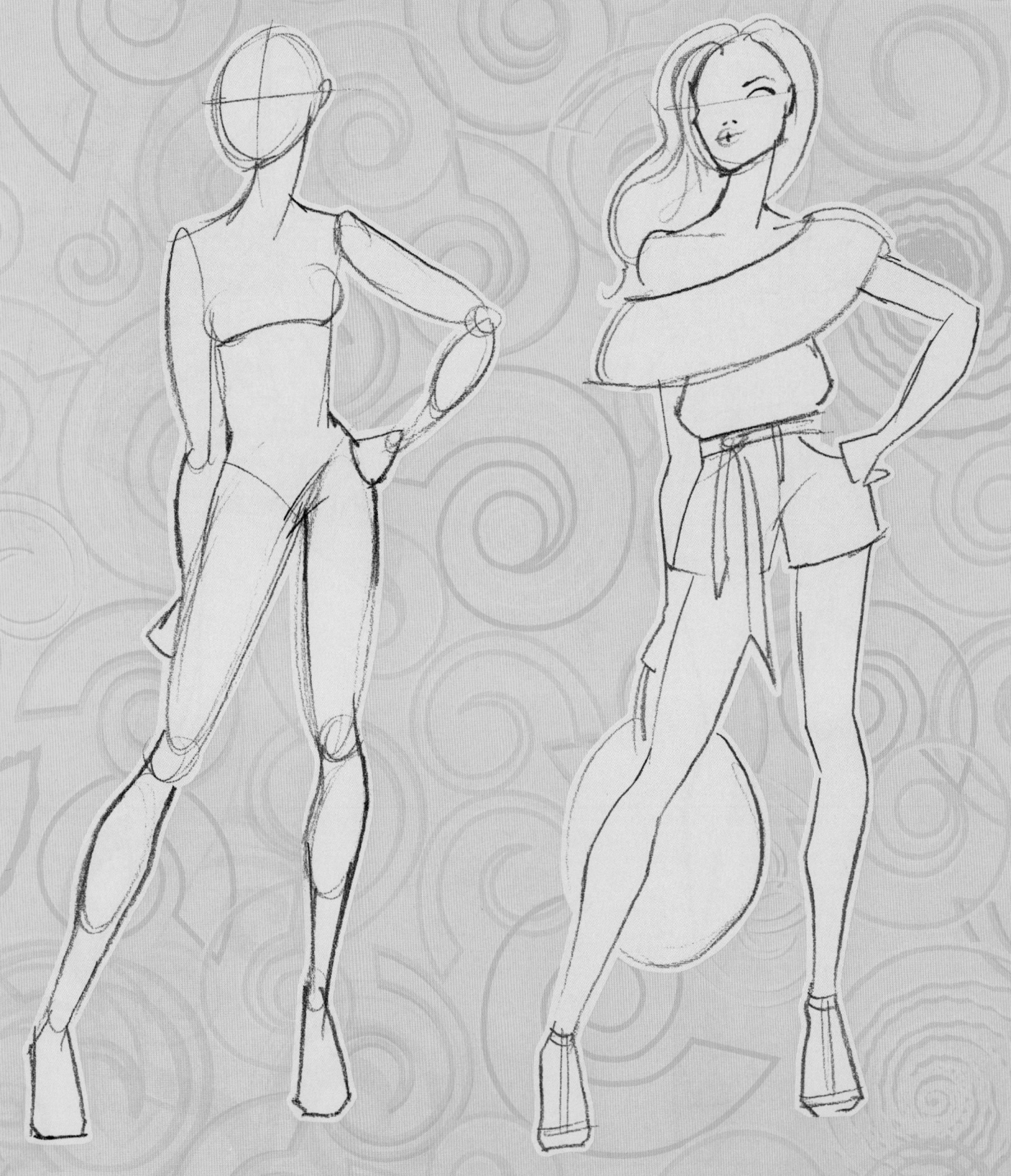

TIP: Lace, ruffles, embroidery, beading, or even sequins will make an even more girly impact.

Pretty Prints

Get noticed with bright prints, colorful bangles, and watermelon-colored wedges. Set the outfit off with a mix of accessories ranging from simple to simply stunning.

TIP: Go beyond geometry by trying out other shapes. Fish, flowers, birds, and fruit are other fun print choices.

Lacy Layers

Girly girls know how to use texture to make their style pop. Lace, embroidery, and faux fur create a rugged yet feminine look. A fedora and oxfords dress up this easy outfit.

TIP: Use white and light blue colored pencils over dark blue watercolors or markers. Bold strokes will give the jeans a bright sheen. Short, lighter strokes will make the jeans look more worn.

Crocheted Cutie

Crochet is a timeless fashion choice for the girly girl. Tights and slouchy gray boots complete a look that's totally casual chic.

TIP: Draw the crochet pattern with white crayon. The crayon wax protects the white paper underneath. Even after being painted over with watercolors, the design stays white. This technique is called resist painting.

TIMELESS TREND

Step back to the past with a retro party dress. Add a modern twist with a silky clutch and some sassy sunglasses. Pearls and bows are timeless additions in any decade.

TIP: Choose vintage colors for this dress. If you don't like mustard, try powder blue, mint green, canary yellow, or ballet pink.

FLOWERS
Are A Girl's Best Friend

Give the girl-next-door image a makeover. A flirty skirt and updated denim add urban appeal. Keep the look sweet with floral and ribbon details.

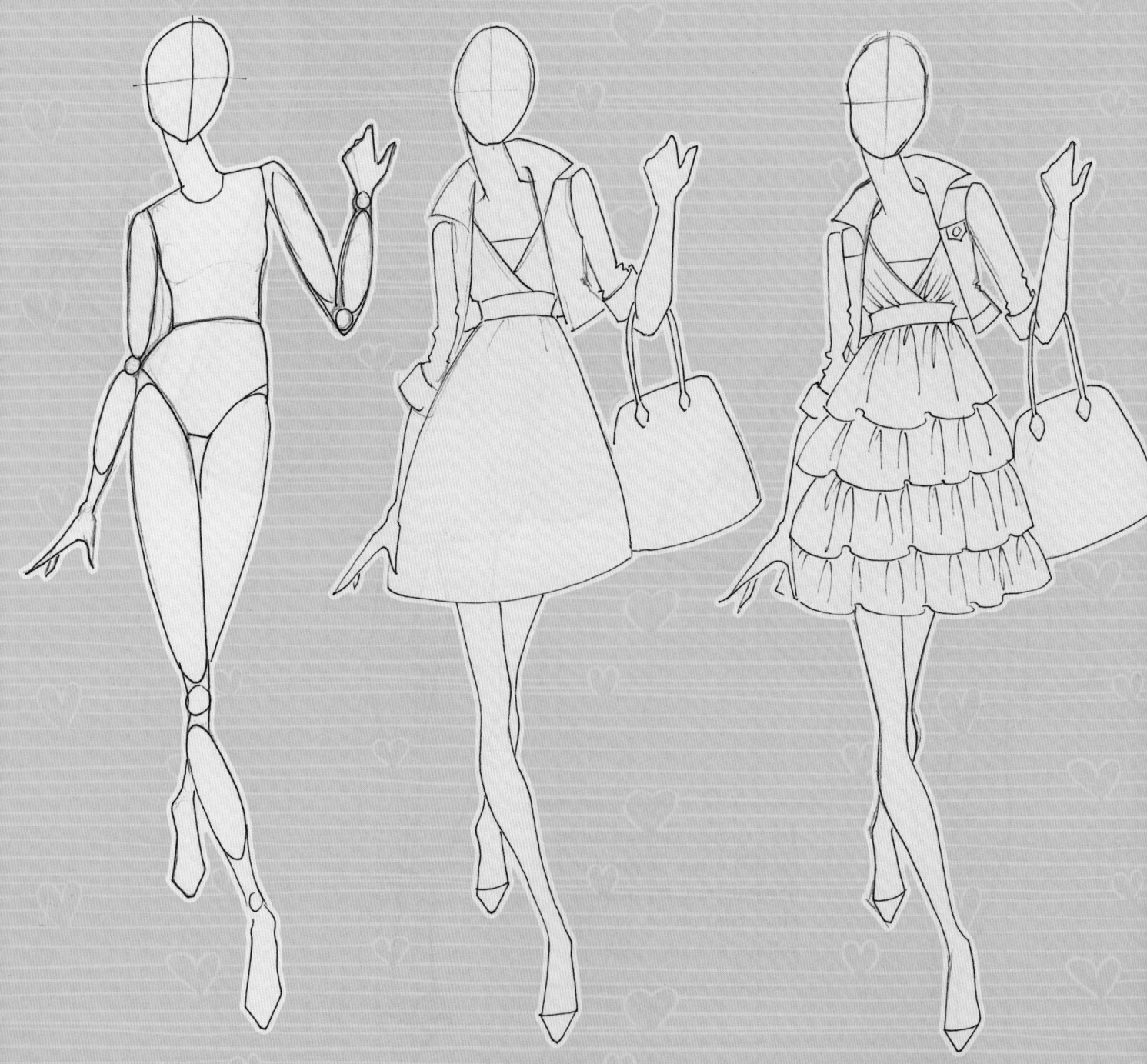

TIP: Use a hair dryer to warm the tips of the colored pencils. This will make it easier to blend the layers of the dress.

Style at Sea

Don't get swept out to sea looking like a shipwreck. Sweep through first class like you're the captain of fashion.

TIP: A white charcoal pencil will add detail to the hat brim.

Cold Weather Cool

The only thing warmer than a girly girl's personality is her cool weather gear. Bundle up, but look good doing it! Add plush pieces to create an outfit that's softer than a snowfall.

TIP: Soft core colored pencils will give the jeans a natural, washed look.

A Vintage Affair

Runways around the world have fallen for the Roaring Twenties. Get familiar with the glitz and glamour of the time period. Then add your own modern girly twist.

TIP: Eyeshadow is a neat tool to use for anything puffy or furry. Use a regular foam applicator and cheap eyeshadow to create the soft lines of the purse.

ON THE RUNWAY

TIP: Regular household products make great blending tools. Try:
- nail polish remover
- rubbing alcohol
- baby oil
- cotton makeup pads
- cotton swabs
- soft fabric or leather

A flouncy white dress is ready for the runway on its own. Get more attention with an over-the-top hat and a blended jacket. Fashion week never looked this good.

CUTE KAWAII

In Japanese, "kawaii" means "pretty" or "cute." This fashion style has a sweet, feminine look without being too girly. A ruffled skirt is set off with belts and bows that give this outfit layers of detail.

TIP: Harajuku style is about layers of clothing working together. Make sure each piece works with the others.

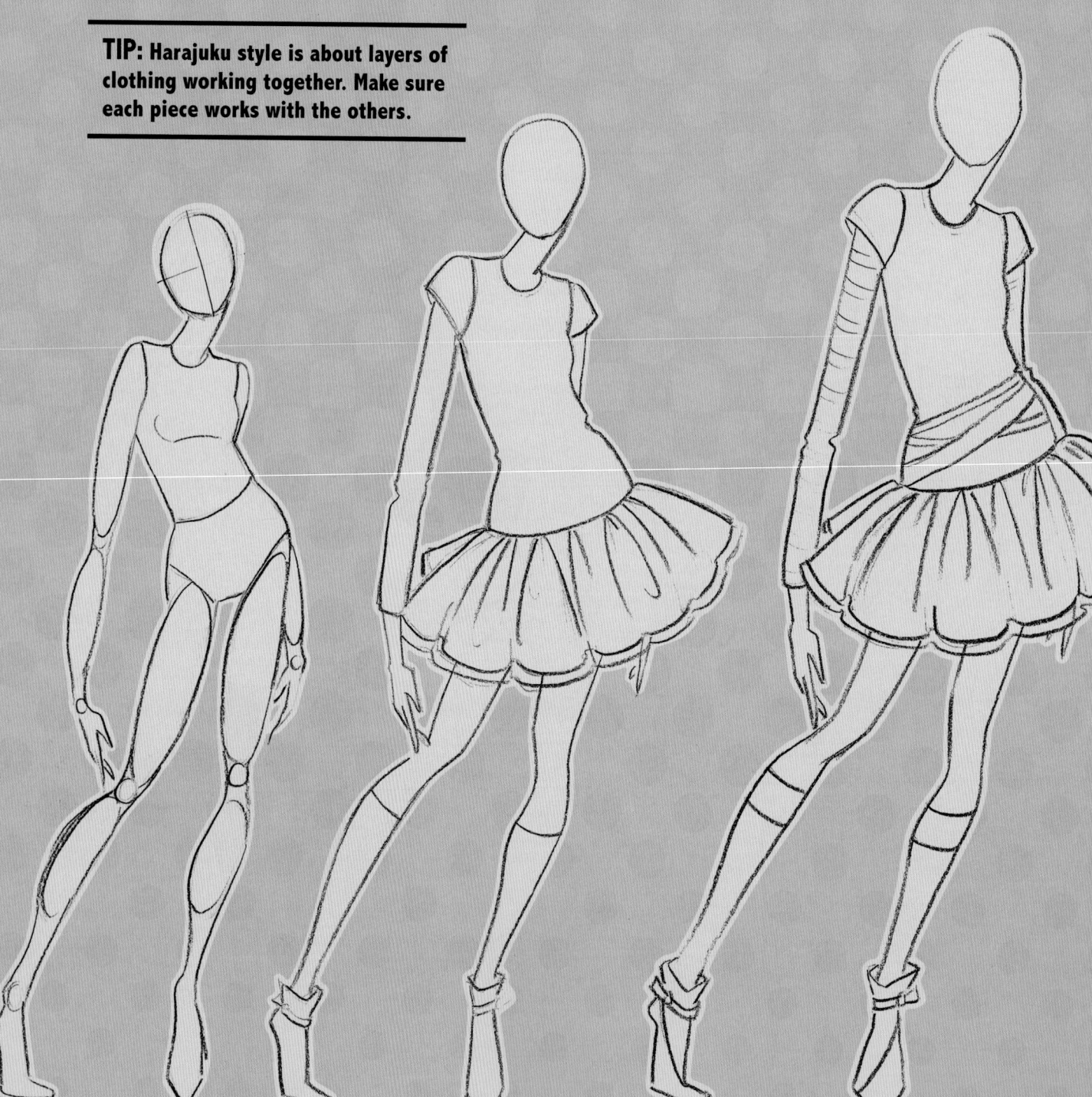

Gothic Girl

Gothic fashion gained fame in America in the late 1990s after celebs were seen sporting black outfits. But Gothic style in Japan was already famous, and is much different. Girlishness and innocence are themes Japanese Goths like to feature.

TIP: Don't get distracted by dark colors. Goth girls are cute and confident!

CYBERPUNK Show-off

Cyberpunk style was first featured in *FRUiTS* magazine in the late 1990s. This style, which combines technology and Gothic fashion, makes the space age look sweet.

TIP: Bright colors, wild prints, and unusual materials bring out the sci-fi side of Harajuku.

Baby, You're Sweet

Frills, lace, and bows are part of the most well-known Harajuku style, known as Loli. A modernized take on elegant, vintage clothing, Loli style brings antique dolls to life.

TIP: Use dark colors instead of light to turn this into a Goth-Loli look.

VISUAL-KEI

Japanese rock bands began adopting the popular Goth-Loli look. Then they incorporated their wardrobes into their music. This style-to-song crossover is called visual-kei.

TIP: In Japanese, visual-kei translates to "visual music style." Extreme makeup and costumes match the dark, creepy music they pair with.

Decora'd Out

Short for "decoration," decora is the most colorful Harajuku style. A rainbow of hues, hair clips, and lots of layers make decora dressers stand out in a crowd.

TIP: Decora is a great style to practice using a variety of colors and tones. Try using a combination of colored pencils, markers, and crayons.

Elegant Loli

Emphasize the Goth half of Goth-Loli with serious colors and romantic ruffles. Ribbons, bows, frills, curls, and lace make a dark, Gothic outfit soft and flirty.

TIP: The layers and frills of this outfit are perfect for practicing shading techniques.

MIXED TRADITIONS

The origin of Harajuku style was the combination of traditional Japanese clothing with Western style. Some call this style "wamono." Kimonos are updated with American-style fabrics and prints. Modern accessories finish the crossover between past and present.

TIP: Go crazy with prints! Animal prints, plaids, polka dots, ginghams, and floral patterns will set off this original outfit.

MR. URA-HARA

"Ura" means "under" in Japanese. The name *Ura-Hara* signifies the reserved, underground aspect of this Harajuku style. Ura-Hara is a combination of hip-hop, graffiti, and skater trends. It is Harajuku's take on male fashion.

TIP: Keep your outfits stylish with clean lines and simple pieces. Use limited color and patterns. Instead, try using unusual fabrics and textures, such as animal fur, spray paint, and metals.

Sweet as a Loli-Pop

Pair the lovely look of Loli with bubblegum pink decora. Combining the two styles creates the cutest kawaii outfit ever! There's no such thing as too much pink when you're sweet as a Loli-pop.

TIP: This outfit will test your creativity! How many accessory pieces can you add before you can't think of any more?

TAKE IT TO THE STREET

A true Harajuku wearer is comfortable standing out in a crowd. Take it to the street by combining punk, kawaii, decora, and visual-kei styles. You'll be stepping out in a one-of-a-kind outfit.

TIP: Experiment with a small combination of colors to find complementary groupings. Try blue, teal, black, and white, or red, purple, white, and yellow.

Belle of the Disco Ball

Dance the night away with a flowing chiffon dress. The blending of color creates a unique, one-of-a-kind gown that shines both on and off the dance floor.

TIP: Pastel pencils are the perfect tool to draw this dress's pattern. The tips create distinctive lines of color. Pastels also blend well, giving the dress a soft look.

Short and Sweet

Ring in the new year with noisemakers, fireworks, and a rocking party dress. Your only resolution should be to look this good next year too!

TIP: This dress's simplicity means it's great to experiment with. Give charcoal or graphite pencils a try instead of regular colored pencil or marker.

Red Carpet Ruffles

Catch the camera's attention while walking the red carpet. Shining ruffles will catch the paparazzi's eye and make the front-page news.

TIP: A metallic marker or white graphite pencil will help the dress shine.

Smooth METALS

Outshine any award with a dress as fluid as liquid metal. Nothing goes with a gold statue like a molten metal dress.

TIP: Use watercolors to color the dress. Sprinkle salt onto wet watercolor wherever you want to add shine. Once the paint has dried, carefully brush off the salt. The salt will create the textured effect on the dress.

STAR-STUDDED SHEATH

A sheath dress flatters most body types. This style also adds a touch of old-fashioned elegance to any formal event. While no necklace is needed, chandelier earrings bring just the right touch of glam.

TIP: Sheath dresses look good with many kinds of necklines. V-neck, halter, strapless, plunging, one-shoulder, and sleeved tops all work with a sheath dress.

21st Century Princess

A modern princess doesn't need Prince Charming to escort her anywhere. Whether on the way to a movie premiere or stopping off at the prom, the Hollywood princess is her own hero.

TIP: Study classic movie princess gowns and combine them with modern trends. You'll come up with something timeless and worthy of red-carpet royalty.

Floral Formal

Who needs a corsage when you've brought your own bouquet? Roses are seen as a symbol of love and beauty, and so should you.

TIP: Use more than one art medium to create the two different hues of red. Color the top of the dress with marker. Draw the roses with watercolors or watercolor pencils.

Hall of Famer

TIP: Stick to simple colors for the accessories. The dress is colorful enough on its own.

A rocker in the hall of fame has reached the height of stardom! Dress like you're at the top even if you're still on the waiting list. This outfit will dazzle any crowd.

Glitz and Gauze

Dressing up can make you feel like you're walking on air. Add a glitzy haze to your outfit with layers of soft chiffon. Then light the way with crystals and a few sparkling jewels.

TIP: To make this outfit really pop, glue small rhinestones to the dress. A toothpick or jewelry picker is a great tool to place gems.

BACKSTAGE GLAM

Presenters and musical acts are essential to the success of any awards show. Have the audience cheering for an encore with this fabulous dress.

TIP: Use a thin-tipped black, blue, or silver permanent marker to outline the dress's layers.

Think Pink

Being a starlet is all about youth and energy. Act your age in a short sweetheart dress with a ruffled hemline. A contrasting chiffon scarf catches the eye and adds a pop of color.

TIP: Use watercolors for the dress. While the paint is wet, add color to the skirt. Once the paint is dry, paint the jewels onto the bodice.

TIP: If you find you like Asian-inspired dresses, add them to your sketchbook. Use Asian prints to put a twist on the ordinary prom dress.

ASIAN INSPIRED

Dress designs and prints from around the world freshen up the formal scene. Traditional Japanese clothing lends itself to bright colors and modern prints. Updated accessories, such as hair ornaments and umbrellas, are tickets to the international stage.

POWER BALLAD

Animal print and ripped denim have been fashion picks for rock stars of any era. Rock the ages with these timeless threads.

TIP: Use whites and very light blues to recreate distressed denim.

SCHOOL OF ROCK

Dress for success at the school of hard knocks. Bring some rock star flair to the boring world of suits and ties. Red accents bring this outfit to a whole new level.

TIP: When it comes to red, a little can go a long way. Use it to enhance the outfit's colors without letting it take over.

Little Miss METALHEAD

Steal the show with big splashes of color. Accessories are what makes this outfit pop. Belts, bangles, and boots hold everything together.

TIP: Metallic tones help the accessories in this outfit stand out. Try using metallic paint instead of regular pens for a look that shines.

LET'S SHRED

Rock stars have to look good any time, any where. Paparazzi could be waiting around any corner! Take style over the edge with a shredded dress and spikes to match.

TIP: Pale colors look great with metallic accents. Instead of silver, try copper, gold, or gunmetal gray.

CROSSOVER ARTIST

Launch the rock star wardrobe to new levels with a fresh look. Keep rocker cred with military-inspired style and bright colors. Plaids lend a touch of everyday fashion to the look.

TIP: Glow-in-the-dark paint will add an extreme effect to the boots and shirt.

ROCK ROYALTY

Some become stars by twists of fate. Others are born famous. Rock royalty dresses like there's a concert happening every night.

TIP: Give the jacket a real leather look by using soft matte colors.

HARD ROCK RIFFS

Storm the stage with star power! Zippers, spikes, and metal feel feminine with the addition of purple and bright green. Sing your heart out, and shout your style out loud.

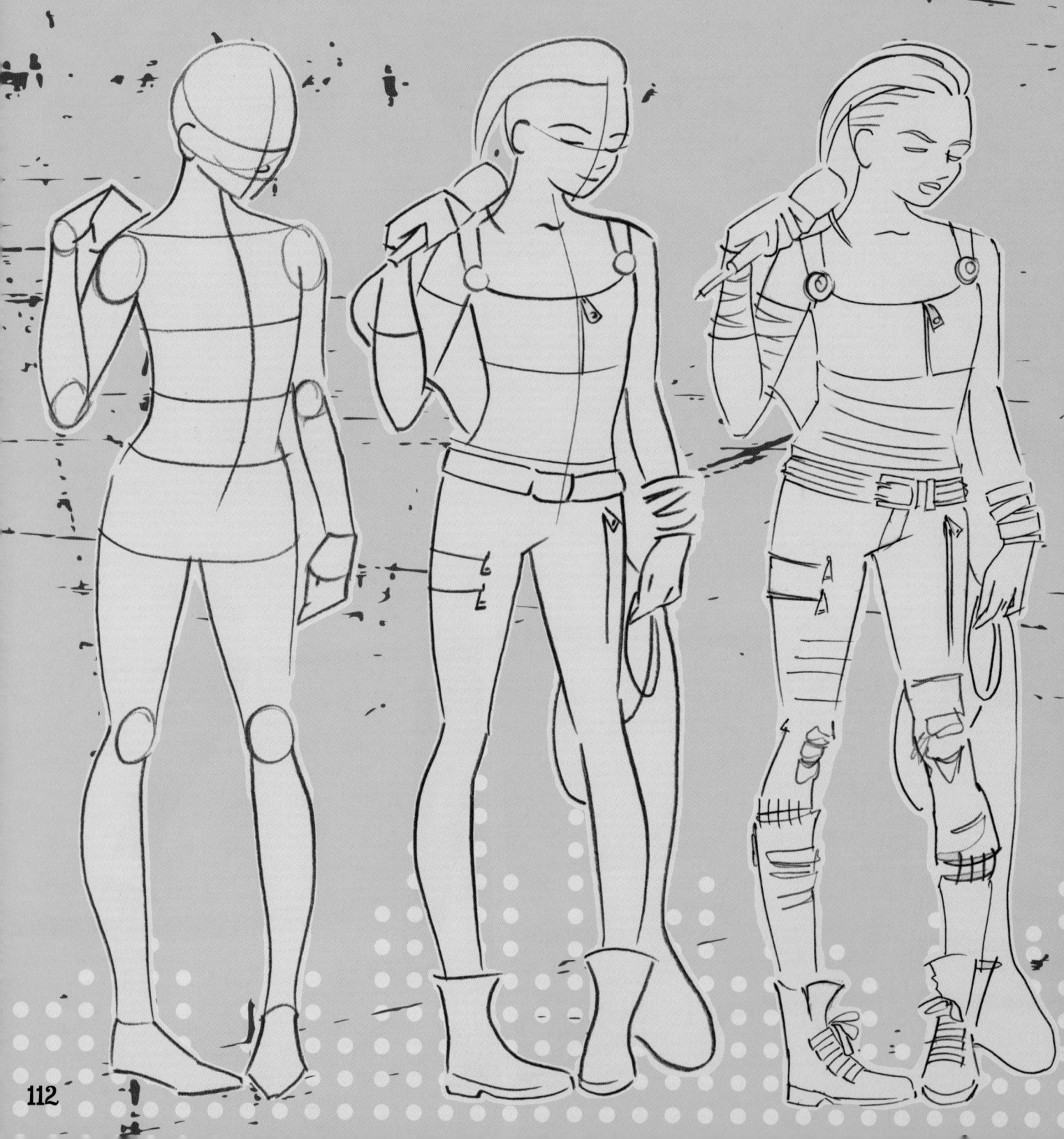

112

TIP: Colored pencils, pastel pencils, or thin-tipped permanent markers will help the plaid pants pop.

113

SOFT METAL

Not all rock stars love studs and metal. Some stars have a softer shine! Add some truly girly flair with a ruffled skirt and a lace top.

TIP: Watercolor pencils will give you the soft, flowy look of the skirt. Use them lightly to copy the pattern on the lace shirt too.

115

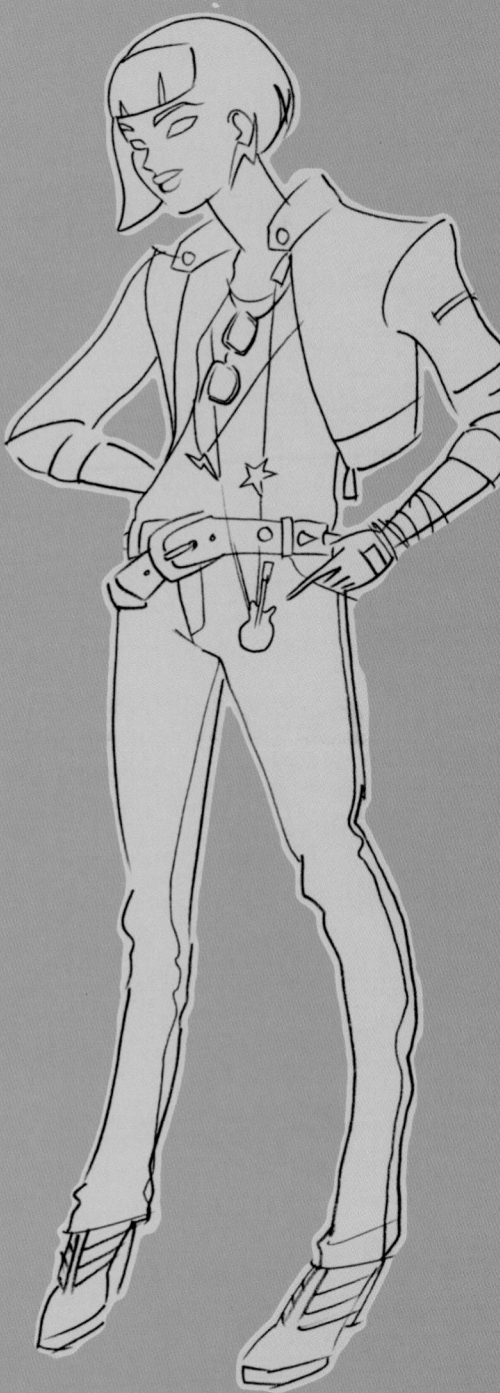

COVER ARTIST

Choosing a great outfit is as important to a rock star as picking a great song. Killer accessories ensure this collection is more than a one-hit wonder.

TIP: Go wild with patterns! If plain pants aren't your thing, experiment with animal prints, bold stripes, or bright graphics.

Country Solo

Go back to the country with classic cowgirl style. Linen, leather, and country-girl sass guarantee an outfit straight from Nashville's Music Row.

TIP: For extra impact, use a silver pen to add small studs to the jacket. Or add swirly lines to the boots with a turquoise marker.

119

PARTY IN THE DARK

Light up the night in a neon-inspired gown. The bright rings will guarantee that this rock star's glow doesn't go out.

TIP: Use scratchboard with rainbow colors underneath for a realistic effect. Etch the design onto the scratchboard. The rainbow colors will make up the lines of the dress.

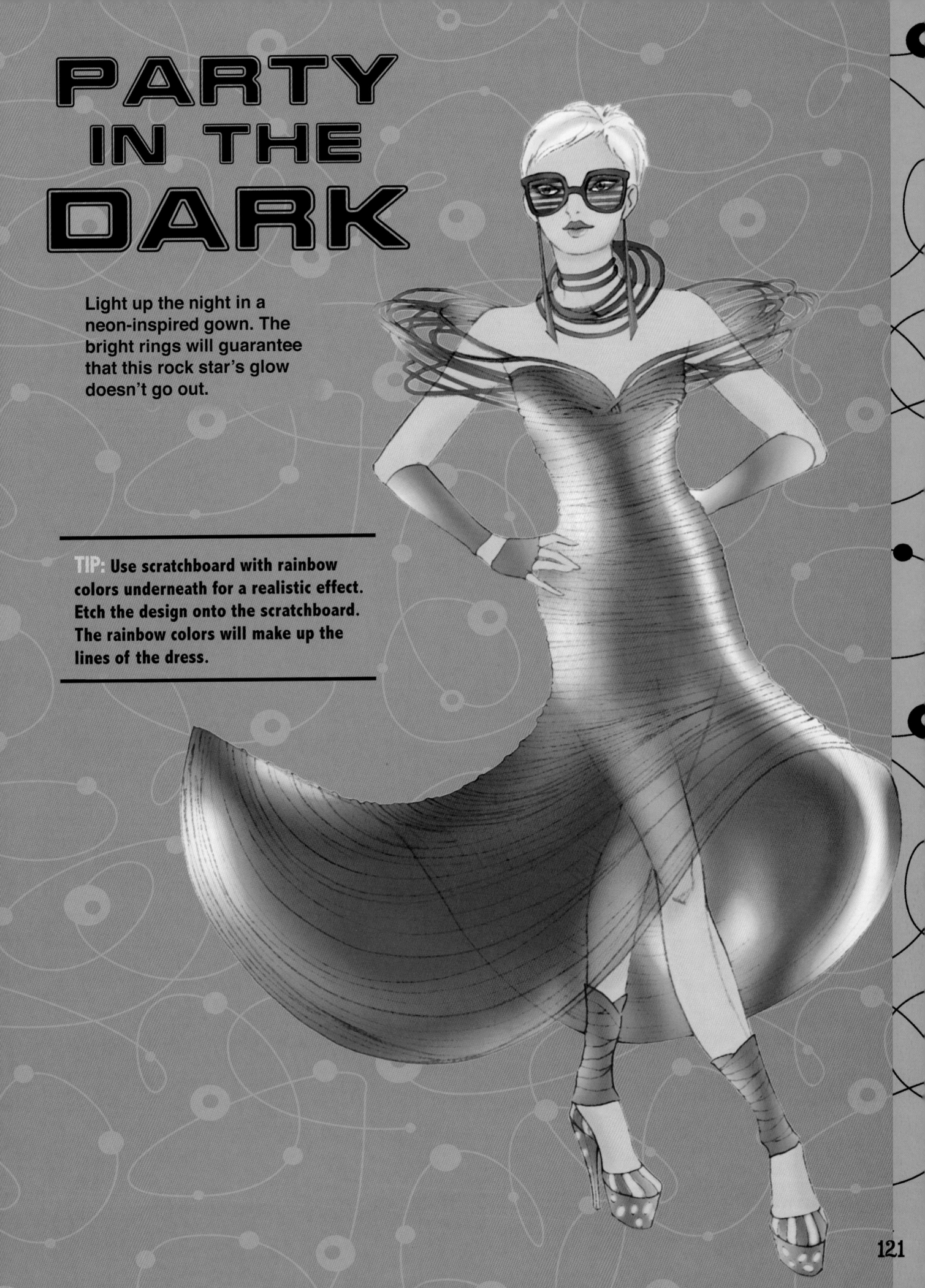

Back to Basics

Start simple with blue jeans and layered tanks. Stick to relaxed fit clothing and sensible accessories. The skater chic style is all about being comfortable in what you wear.

TIP: Use shading to add creases and depth to the shirts and pants.

VERT STYLE

A trucker hat, boyfriend sweater, and awesome jeans are all you need to reach the height of skater chic.

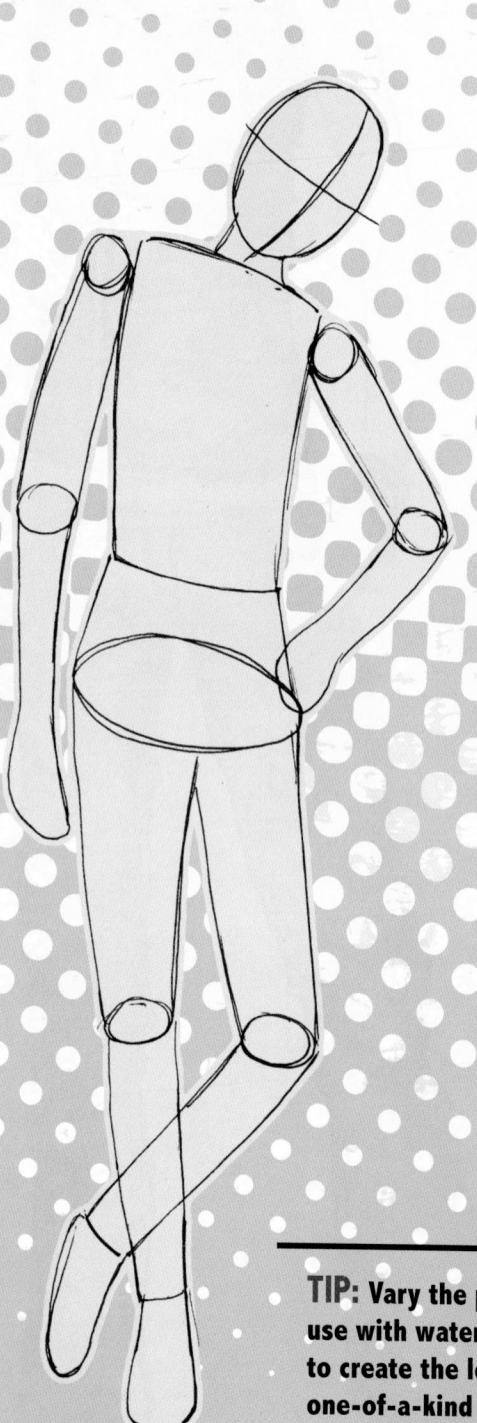

TIP: Vary the pressure you use with watercolor pencils to create the look of these one-of-a-kind jeans.

STREET LEAGUE STYLE

The skater boy is as casual as they come. He's ready to hang with friends on the sidelines or gain big air in a halfpipe. Fashion stays on the down-low with street league style.

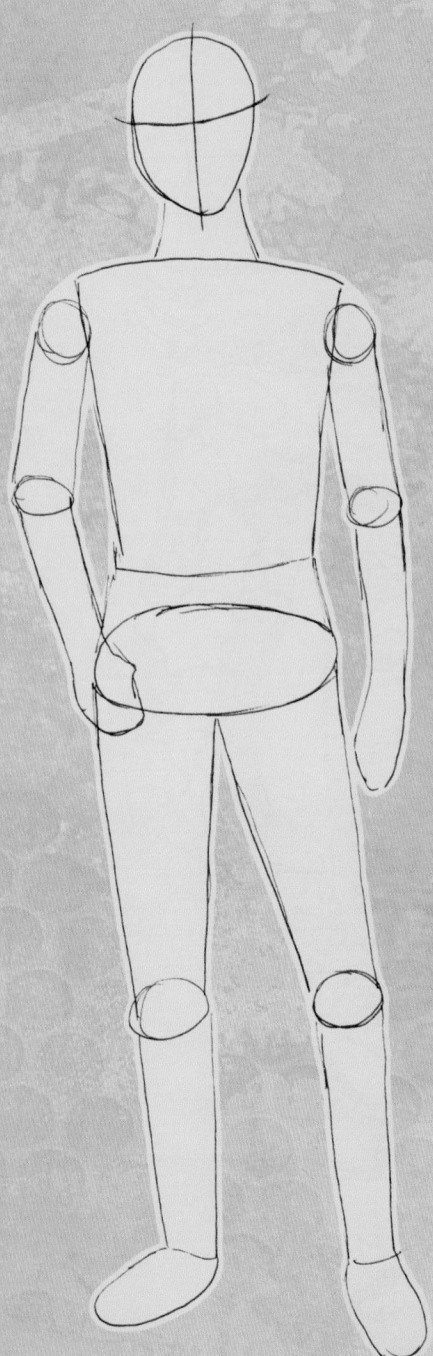
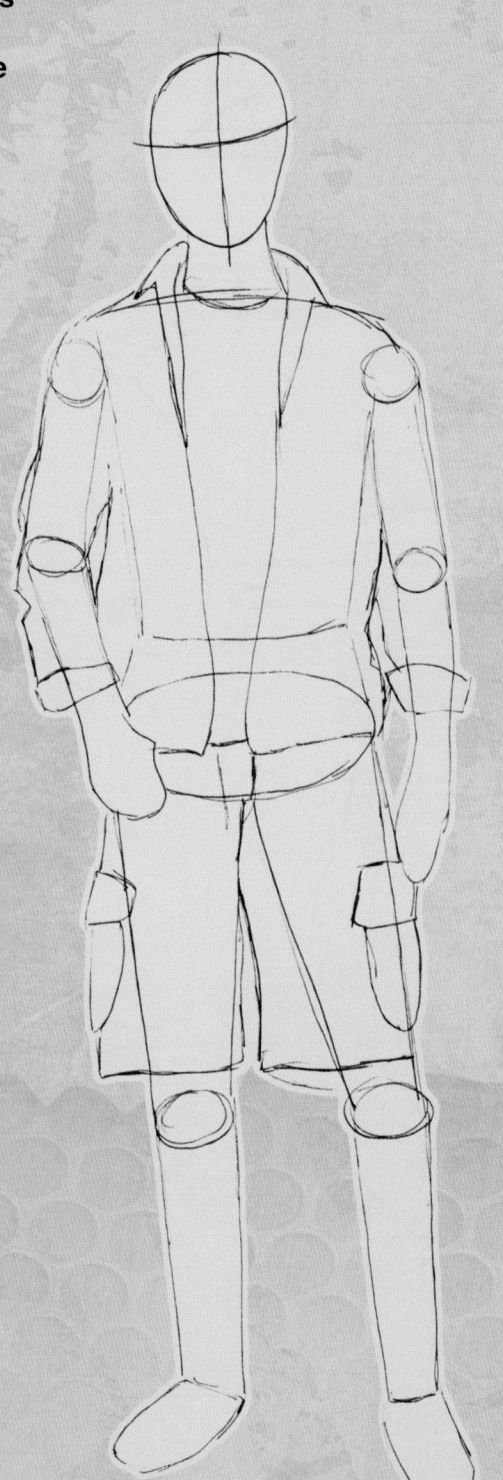

TIP: Plaid is a great pattern for experimenting with color. Try color combinations that you haven't used before.

SKATER PREP

Educate yourself at skater school while looking stylish too. Put a spin on ordinary plaid by adding an underlayer of taffeta and an overlayer of silver chains.

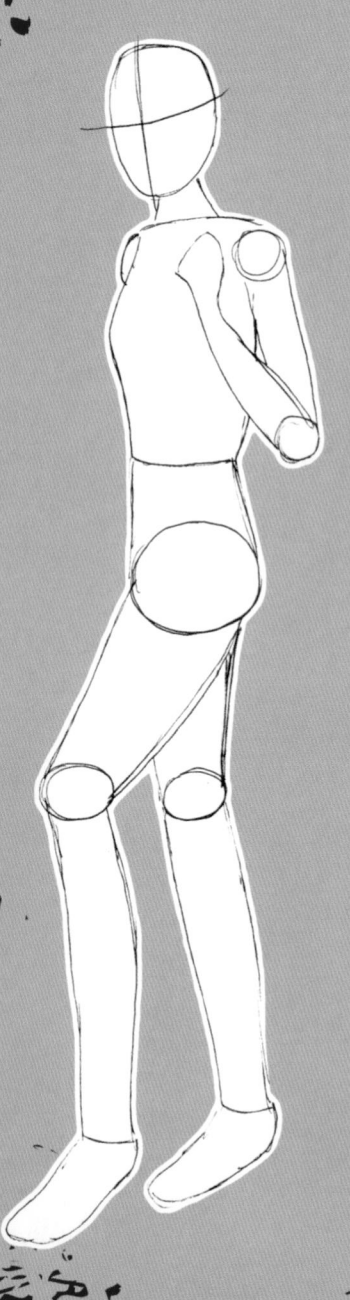
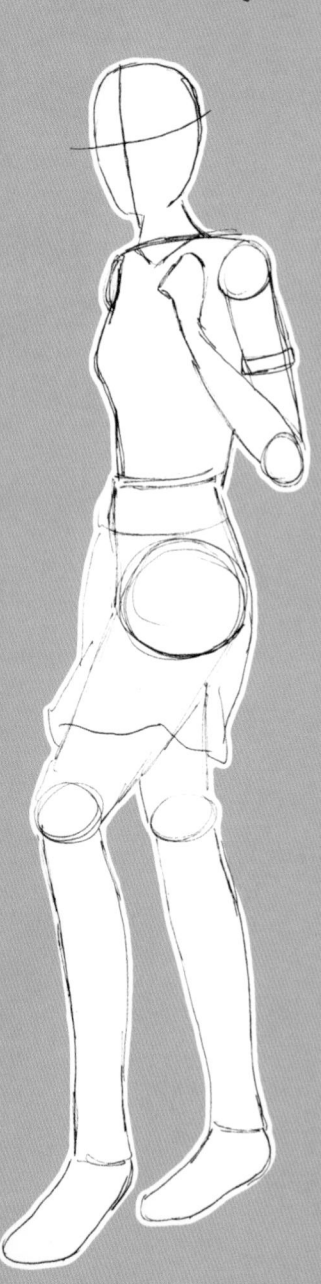

TIP: Try using a cotton swab to soften the lines for a more natural look. Moisten the cotton swab for a more blended pattern.

SURF SKATER

When skater girls need sun, they hit the beach and surf the boardwalk! Wave to the crowd in style while wearing natural tones of the earth and sea.

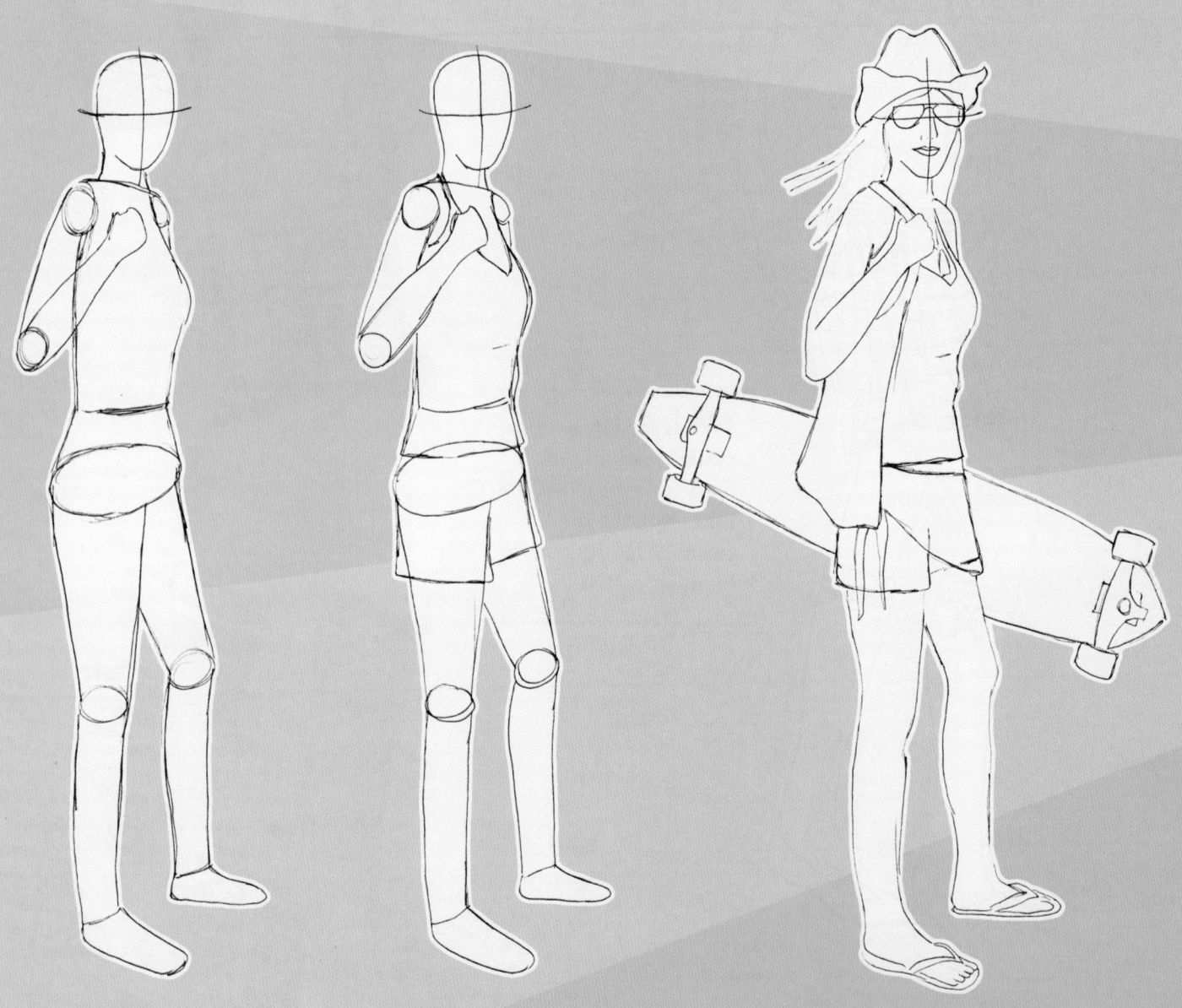

TIP: Keep your pencil lines short and jagged. This will give your sketch a more rugged feel.

Hanging Out

Get relaxed with skater chic casual wear. Dress up familiar jeans with a super stylish hoodie. Add coordinating sunglasses and a tasseled bag. Then top things off with a knit hat. Hanging out never looked so good!

TIP: Use both white and dark gray paints to add shading and dimension to the distressed jeans.

TOP DECK STYLE

Skater guys have a sense of style too! Keep it simple with casual pants and a tee. Give the outfit a personal twist with a colorful coat, a pair of shoes, and a bright belt.

TIP: With its simple lines, this outfit can be tailored to fit your own personal style.

Overall Impression

Skater girls don't spend all day at the skate park. For more dressy occasions, a sundress, boots, and denim jacket will take the stylish skater anywhere she pleases.

TIP: Use watercolor pencils to create the dress print. Color in the pattern, and then brush gently with a wet paintbrush. Once the pattern is dry, use a black pen to add more texture.

TIP: Try using the watercolor pencils on a wet surface. See which technique you like better.

Supertech Sparkle

Get ready to go out by adding a shimmery sparkle. Start with an animal print skirt as a centerpiece. Then add a few pieces of interest that catch the eye.

TIP: Experiment with texture! Glue down a piece of fabric in place of the skirt. Or use glitter glue for some 3-D shine.

1080 Winter Wear

Staying warm while gliding through snow is important. Looking good while doing it is also key! Turn heads on the hill with gear that's snowboarder chic.

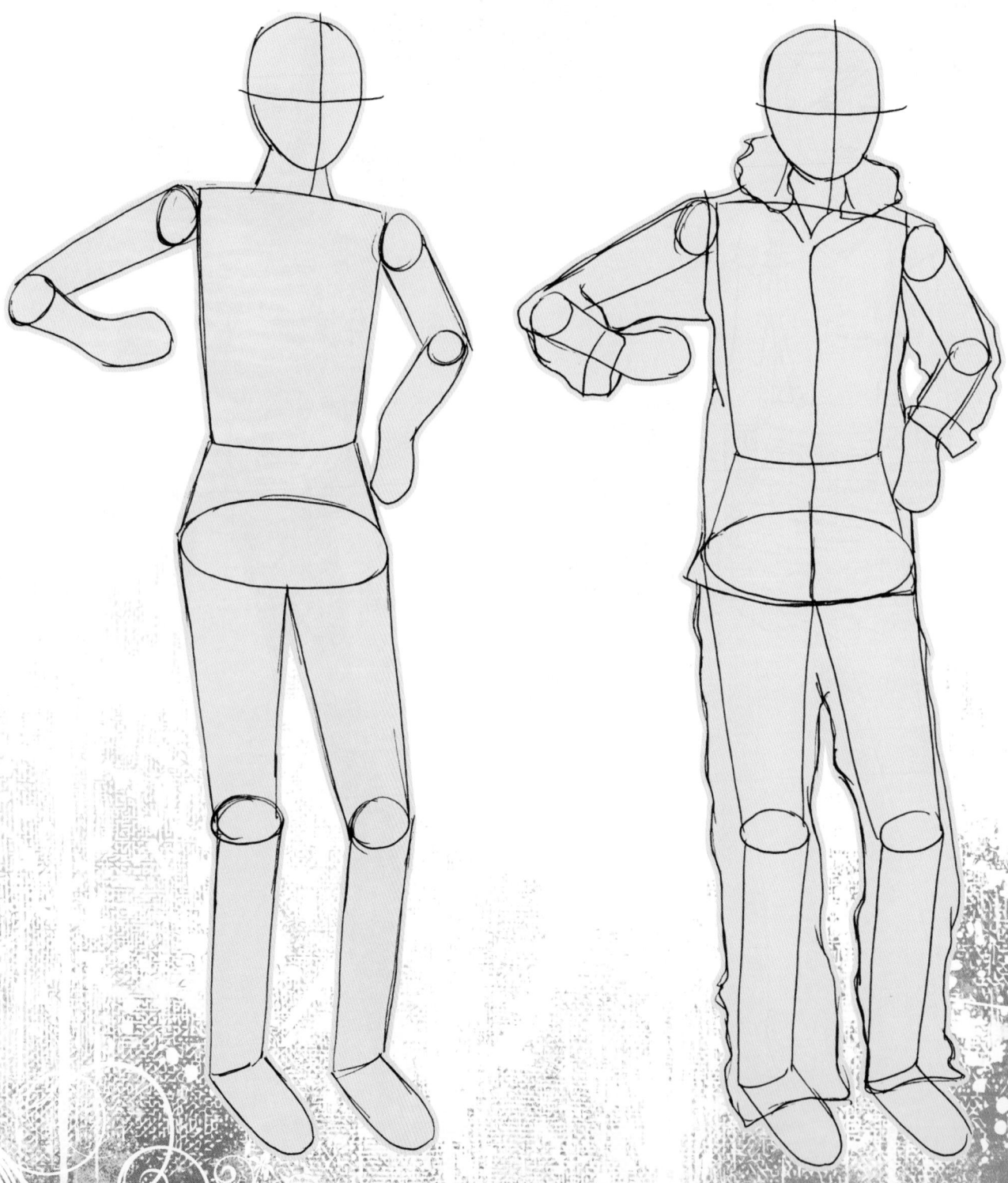

At thePARK

Dress to impress at the skate park! Hi-top boots, a practical-but-fashionable outfit, and a helmet will get you noticed. Grab a board, and you're ready to go.

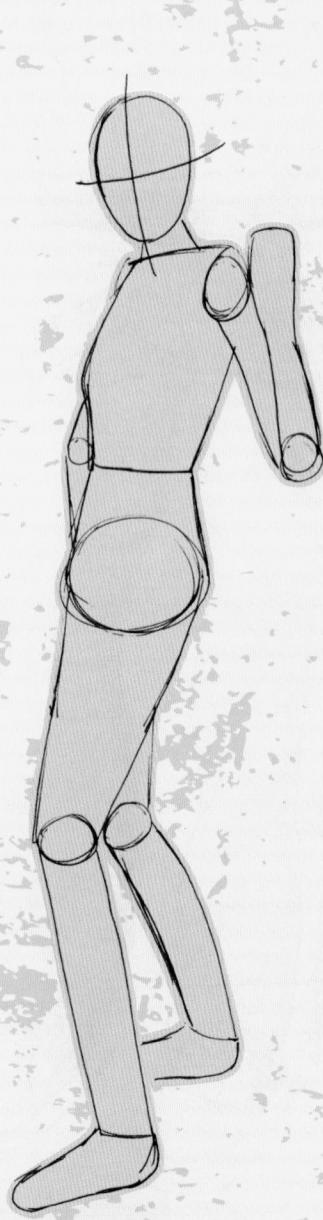
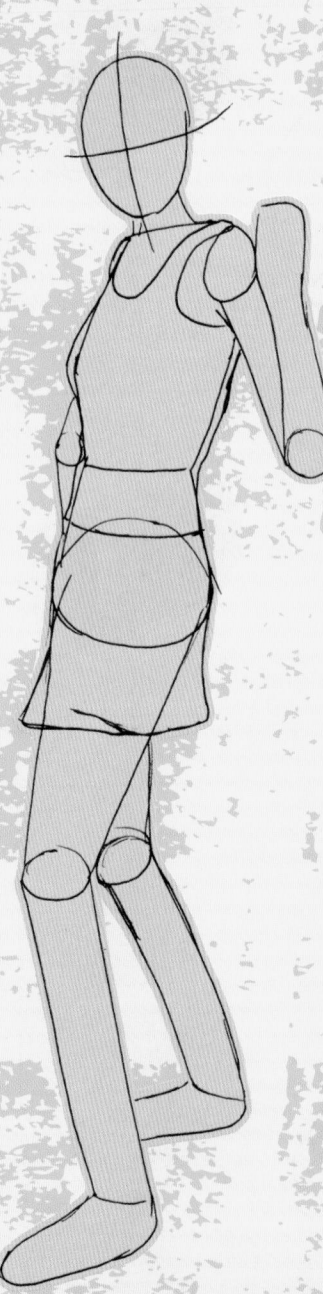

TIP: Turn safety gear into an accessory! Coordinate outfits with helmets, goggles, gloves, and protective pads.

Written By
Mari Bolte

Illustrated By
Sole Otero (*All-American Girl*), Brooke Hagel (*Girly Girl* and *Harajuku*),
Sarah Dahl (*Hollywood* and *Rock Star*), and Jennifer Rzasa (*Skater Chic*)

Designer
Lori Bye

Art Director
Nathan Gassman

Production Specialist
Laura Manthe

Capstone Young Readers are published by Capstone,
1710 Roe Crest Drive, North Mankato, Minnesota 56003
www.capstoneyoungreaders.com

Library of Congress Cataloging-in-Publication Data
Bolte, Mari.
  Fashion drawing studio : a guide to sketching stylish fashions / by Mari Bolte.
    pages cm — (Capstone young readers. Drawing fun fashions)
  Summary: "Lively text and fun illustrations describe how to draw cool fashions"—Provided by publisher.
  ISBN 978-1-62370-005-8 (paperback)
  1. Fashion drawing—Juvenile literature. I. Title.
  TT509.B652 2013
  741.6'72—dc23   2012028361

The illustrations in this book were created with colored pencils, ink, markers, watercolors, and digitally.
Design elements by Shutterstock.

Printed in China.
012014   007954R